# Missouri State Capitol

## Jefferson City

## Jane Moorman

There is a saying, "It was a Friday night, and it seemed like a good idea at the time." That sums up the beginning of the State Capitols Project.

When photographer Jane Moorman told her brother of her idea of photographing state capitols, he said, "You do know there are 50 states and two of them you can't drive to."

Her answer was, "Your point is? It gives me a good reason to visit every state."

# Missouri Capitol Reflects the State's People

Thomas Jefferson



After the Louisiana Purchase, the Missouri Territory was organized in 1812.

With the migration of settlers into the region, the government seat moved from along the Mississippi River inland to a village first called Lohman's Landing.

When the legislature decided to relocate there, they proposed the name "Missouriopolis" before settling on the "City of Jefferson" to honor Thomas Jefferson, who was the United States President when the region was purchased from France.

Over the years, the city was most often referred to as Jefferson City, and the name stuck. It is also referred to as Jeff City.

Located on the Missouri River in the center of the state, the current Missouri State Capitol is the fourth to house the state's government.

Fire destroyed two previous capitols prior to the construction of the Roman Renaissance building that was completed in 1918.

The design by architects Egerton Swartwout and Evarts Tracy was chosen from 69 entries in the contest for the honor.

After the capitol was built, it was recommended that attention be turned toward decorating the marble structure. A commission was appointed in 1917, and funding was provided for artists to be commissioned to create artwork for the interior.

At the dedication of the capitol on Oct. 6, 1924, Gov. Arthur Hyde spoke of the commission's achievement.

He stated that adorning the capitol with noble works of art made the building a memorial of the history, achievement and aspirations of a great people, creating not just a building but a shrine for the lovers of history and art.

Besides the art in the capitol's rotunda, there are lunettes in the hallways that are scenes to illustrate the history, resources and ambitions of the state.

One area that has grown since its conception in 1982 is the Hall of Famous Missourians.

There are 50-plus bronze busts of honorees from all walks of life, including artists, athletes, activists, politicians, inventors, decorated military members and entrepreneurs.

Within this book, only a few are displayed; however, a book has been created for just the honorees.

# Missouri Statehouse Overlooks the Missouri River

The present capitol building, completed in 1917, stands high atop a bluff overlooking the Missouri River.

Designed by architects Egerton Swartwout and Evarts Tracy, the structure is a classical design of symmetry and elegance and is one of the last statehouses constructed in the Roman Renaissance style.

The design reflects the period known as the American Renaissance, a time of political and cultural activity influenced by Greek and Roman classicism.

South view of the capitol.

The building's exterior is made of limestone from Carthage, Missouri.

The floors of all the corridors, the rotundas and the treads of the stairways are the same marble.

The third floor contains stone from the Phenix Quarry in Greene County, Missouri.

At the south entrance to the building stand bronze doors measuring 13 feet by 18 feet, which open at the exterior grand stairway.

West view of the capitol.

# Dome

The capitol's Baroque dome is loosely modeled after St. Peter's Basilica in Rome. The marble dome features 16 carved panels around its diameter, which add a pinkish accent to the dome. Each pane is five feet by nine feet.

# Ceres

Ceres rules over the capitol 260 feet above the ground. The goddess of grain was chosen to symbolize the state's great agricultural history. It was sculpted by Sherry Fry.

The bronze statue, weighing 1,407 pounds, was installed on Oct. 29, 1924. It has been struck by lightning more than 300 times.

# Jefferson Welcomes Visitors

A 13-foot bronze statue of Thomas Jefferson, the creation of sculptor James Earle Fraser, graces the south entrance of the capitol.

# Portico

*Salus Populi Suprema Lex Esto* is etched into the façade of the south portico. The Latin phrase "Let the welfare of the people be the supreme law" also appears on the state seal.

Eight 48-foot columns support the south portico, while six 40-foot columns support the north portico.

There are 134 columns in the building, one-fourth of the stone used in the entire structure.

# Sculptures

Adolph Alexander Weinman sculpted the figures in the pediment over the south portico.

The north façade is embellished by a frieze sculpted by Herman Atkins MacNeil illustrating the history of Missouri, a theme continued on the south façade by artist Alexander Stirling Calder.

# Rotunda Dome

A huge bronze chandelier weighing 9,000 pounds hangs from the dome's oculus, 171 feet above the first floor. The paintings of Frank Brangwyn on the oculus, panels and pendentive of the dome are visible from the ground floor.

The artwork in the dome's oculus are allegorical depictions of commerce, agriculture, science and art, which are repeated in the rotunda's first-floor art.

# Rotunda Floor

Bronze statues of Meriwether Lewis and Williams Clark flank the rotunda stairway on the first floor.

The rotunda marble floor features a bronze state seal inlaid into the stone.

William Clark

Meriwether Lewis

# Grand Staircase to Second Floor

# Rotunda Art

Missouri's capitol boasts a two-story rotunda atrium that features murals by Frank Brangwyn. The third floor features pendentive murals also by Brangwyn.

Brangwyn believed that art should be as widely accessible as possible, or at least "within reach of discriminating person of moderate means," rather than restricted to a wealthy elite. He believed an artist's mission was "to decorate life."

As an internationally renowned artist-craftsman, Brangwyn created more than 12,000 designs and works in the form of murals, oil and watercolor paintings, ceramics, textiles, tapestries, carpets, posters, stained glass, wood carving, and prints.

# Frank Brangwyn's Murals

Frank Brangwyn's eight murals on the lower level of the rotunda are allegoric depictions of art, education, science, commerce, earth, water, fire and air. The murals symbolize the euphoria that Americans felt as an emerging world power after World War I.

# Pendentive Murals by Frank Brangwyn

*The Historic Landing*

*The Pioneers*

*The Home Makers*

*The Builders*

# Governor's Reception Room

The Governor's Reception Room features murals of Missourians who made significant contributions in the fields of education and literature. Among them are Susan Blow, founder of the first public kindergarten; Eugene Field, best known for his children's poetry; James S. Rollins, known as the 'Father of the University of Missouri,' and Mark Twain, prominent humorist writer. Gari Melchers, a native of Detroit, Michigan, created the panels measuring 5 feet wide and 12 feet panels.

Circling the room above the windows are carved wood seals for each state in the union.

# House of Representatives Chamber

The *Glory of Missouri in War* painting by French artist Charles Hoffbauer in 1922, depicts Missouri troops traveling through a war-torn area of France on their way to the front during World War I. It is 49-feet long by 21-feet high.

# H.T. Schladermundt's Stained-Glass Windows

Above the speaker's dais is a large mosaic glass window titled The *Glory of Missouri in Peace.* In the center of the window stands a female representing Missouri, flanked by symbols of commerce, mining, agriculture, justice, art and science.

Windows surrounding the chamber depict elements of democracy, including honor, truth, progress, virtue, charity, family, morality, temperance, liberty and equality.

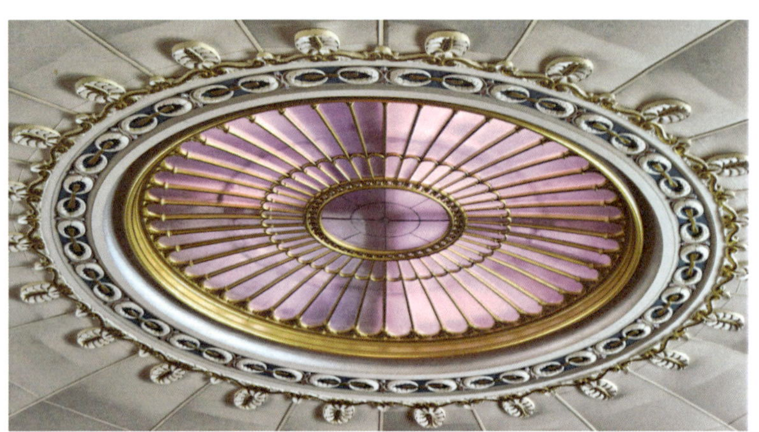

SALVS POPVLI SVPREMA LEX ESTO

SALVS POPVLI SVPREMA LEX

LIBERTY
EQUALITY

# Senate Chamber

The Senate Chamber is not open for visitors, even if you take a guided tour.

Inside are four murals by Richard E. Miller depicting four time periods in the state's development: The Colonial Period with *Daniel Boone at the Judgement Tree*; The Territorial Period with *Jefferson greeting Lewis and Clark*; The Civil War Era with *Blair's Speech at Louisiana, Missouri*; and The Era of Westward Expansion with *Benton's Speech at St. Louis*.

There are quotes carved into the marble walls between the murals. The murals were painted in 1915.

The artwork also includes a painted window titled *Hernando DeSoto Lands In America*, depicting European exploration of the New World. The scene illustrates the beginning of DeSoto's historic expedition with Native Americans standing on the shore awaiting his arrival.

Sixteen towering columns support the ceiling. The columns stand atop polished walls made of Carthage Marble blocks taken from the Phenix Quarry in Green County. The columns are made of polished New Hampshire marble.

# Thomas Hart Benton's Missouri Mural

Thomas Hart Benton was commissioned in 1935 to paint a mural on the four walls of the House of Representative Lounge.

The 40-foot mural "*A Social History of the State of Missouri*" was completed in 18 months.

Visitors to the Capitol can view the murals only during a guided tour.

Benton chose to depict the character of Missourians in the role they played in the development of the state. More realistic than what politicians desired, the mural became a source of ridicule and controversy.

The people portrayed were ordinary people, not favorite sons, which caused criticism from legislators.

Among the people portrayed were laborers, settlers, enslaved people and farmers, as well as Jesse James robbing a train, Huck Finn from Mark Twain's novel, and the Frankie and Johnny scene.

Many of the people in the paintings were known to Benton.

In response to legislators' criticism, Benton created a mule/cow by painting the hind section of the mule, pulling a plow as a cow's hind section.

BANK
C&A

Thomas Hart Benton

Benton used a powdered paint material made with raw egg yolks to paint his ordinary people. Known as egg tempera, he painted it directly on the wall instead of on canvass.

Oftentimes, while working on the mural, a visitor would wander in to watch. One occasion, when Benton thought the visitor fit the image he was trying to portray, he would add their face to the mural.

Benton's work is strongly associated with the Midwest United States, the region in which he was born and which he called home for most of his life.

Along with Grant Wood and John Steuart Curry, he was at the forefront of the Regionalist art movement. In the early 1920s, Benton declared himself an "enemy of modernism," he began the naturalistic and representation work known as Regionalism.

# Hall of Famous Missourians

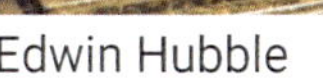
Edwin Hubble

Sacajawea

Harry S. Truman

Charlie Parker

Mark Twain

Walter Cronkite

Susan Blow

John O'Neil

Betty Grable

Walt Disney

Circling the rotunda on the third floor, the Hall of Famous Missourians is displayed between the House of Representatives and Senate chambers.

Since 1982, the state senate has selected Missourians who have contributed to the state's reputation and well-being.

Above the bronze busts are pediment art that honors the people who contributed to the evolution of the state from frontier days to statehood.

# Allen T. True Pediment Art

BVFFALO HVNTER

FREE TRAPPER

A FACTEUR

PIONEER MOTHER

RAILROAD BVILDER

The CATTLEMAN

A RIVER PILOT

The FREIGHTER

The MINER

The MACHINIST

The SCIENTIST

The BVILDER

# Lunette Painting Along Hallways

Members of the Taos Society of Artists painted seventeen lunette paintings depicting scenes of Missouri history.

The subjects included such themes as Missouri settlements, its military contribution to national victories, and its prominent politicians and leaders. Also included were the state's industries, technological achievements and older towns and cities.

*Chouteau's Treaty With The Osages, The First Circuit Court In Boone County,* and *The First Discussion of the Platte Purchase* by Walter Ufer.

*Assembly of the First Legislature, St. Charles, 1821*
by artist Richard E. Miller

*Battle of Sacramento 1847*
by artist Fred. G. Carpenter

*Surrender of the Miamis to Gen. Henry Dodge 1814* by artist Oscar E. Berninghaus.

*Assembly of Calaway's Rangers* by artist Bert Greer Phillips

*The Artery of Trade* by artist Frank B. Nuderscher

*Early Led Mining* by artist Oscar E. Berninghaus

*Battle of Wilson Creek* by artist N.C Wyeth

*Riches of the Mines* by artist Tom P. Barnett

# Bears Are Everywhere

From the state flag and state seal to the capitol's elevators and water fountain, bears are everywhere in the Missouri State Capitol, even on the newel of the grand staircase.

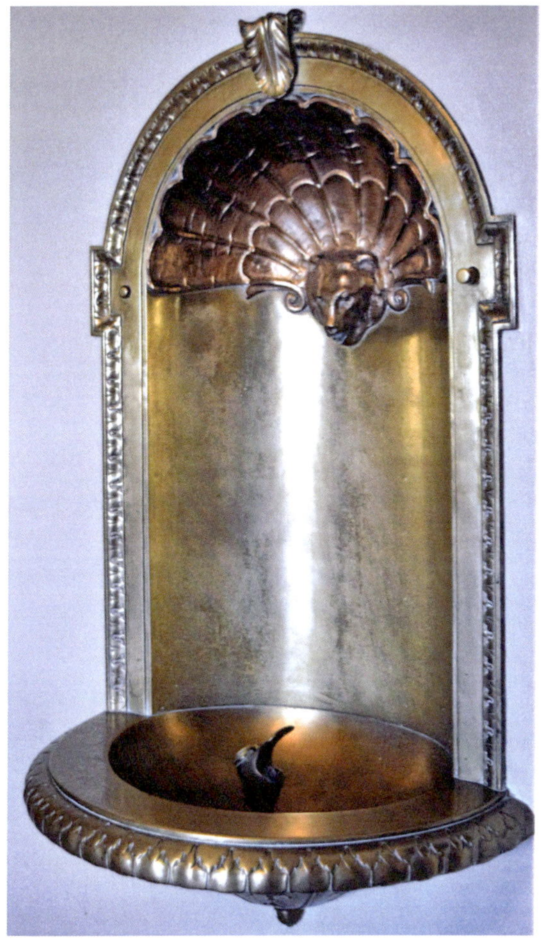

# About the Photographer

Jane Moorman describes herself as an adventurer who loves to drive back roads to see what there is to see.

During her 30-year journalism career, Jane honed her photographic skills as a photojournalist, including covering high school sporting events.

A friend once said, "I wish I could see the world as Jane sees it. Finding the beauty in things that most of us don't take time to see."

She currently lives in Albuquerque, New Mexico, but says her real home is on the road.

# Missouri State Seal

The Great Seal of the State of Missouri was designed by Robert Wells of Jefferson City and was adopted in 1822.

The center of the seal contains the United States Eagle with 13 stars on the right side and, on the left, symbols representing the state: a bear representing strength and bravery, a crescent moon, a symbol of the Virgin Mary and a nod to the French who first settled Missouri, represents the newness of statehood and the potential for growth.

Surrounding these symbols is the motto "United we stand, divided we fall." The belt buckle signifies the state's ability to secede from the union if deemed necessary, i.e., the belt can be unbuckled.

Two bears, representing Missouri's native bears, support this center shield.

A scroll carries the state motto, Salus populi suprema lex esto, a Latin phrase meaning "Let the welfare of the people be the supreme law."

The year 1820 is inscribed in Roman numerals below the scroll, although Missouri was not officially granted statehood until 1821.

Above the shield is a helmet representing Missouri's state sovereignty.

Twenty-four stars grace the top portion of the seal representing Missouri being the 24th state entering the union.

The outer circle of the seal bears the words "The Great Seal of the State of Missouri," with a rope pattern edging the final seal.